MW00618773

# THE STORY OF
# Berkeley Castle
## WHAT'S TRUE AND WHAT'S NOT

# Jeanne Mozier

Published by High Street Press, Berkeley Springs, West Virginia

# Chapters

# Chapter 1

## BERKELEY CASTLE
A True Vision of Romance in Berkeley Springs

Photo courtesy Robert Peak Design

It's inevitable.

People look up from the springs and park in the heart of Berkeley Springs and gasp. There's a real stone castle perched on the side of the western ridge overlooking the famed warm mineral springs and the tiny colonial town established around them.

It's memorable.

Berkeley Castle comes complete with a three-story tower and crenellated parapets trimming the roof in the manner of battlements. There are 15 major interior rooms and a basement "dungeon." A matching stone gatetower was stranded on the opposite side of the state highway when WV9 was cut into the mountainside in the early 1920s.

When you have a castle in town, romantic legends are sure to follow.

It's a magnet for stories of love and heartbreak, decadence and even murder. In the case of Berkeley Castle, many of the stories are completely fabricated, or have specks of truth embellished by tour guides during the mid and late twentieth century. Teasing out fact from fantasy is a challenging exercise but a worthy one. As it happens, the documented facts of the story are as compelling as the structure.

When Samuel Taylor Suit, a businessman of Maryland, began in 1885, "laying the foundation of his cottage" according to the *News*, a local newspaper of the time, the chic Victorian resort community of Berkeley Springs had more than two dozen splendid structures. Work progressed throughout the next year on what the paper called, "one of the finest residences in the state." Made of local sandstone, the structure reportedly gave townspeople, "the impression of a handsome castle nestled among the rocks and cliffs of the mountain." It dominated the noted cottage community of Berkeley Springs.

Under roof by May 1887, it was occupied in late August by Suit, his young third wife, Rosa and their three children. They returned to their winter home in Washington, D.C. in early October.

It is possible that Suit and his family briefly returned to their stone castle in May of 1888. In June, he was taken ill in Washington and died there on October 1. Rosa was 27. Suit's will left her virtually everything, naming her administrator and trustee for the children – provided she never married again.

Over the next decade, Rosa lived a life befitting a rich young widow. Her stone castle with its 17-foot-ceilinged ballroom, paneled dining room and grand stairway of carved walnut was the perfect setting for her many parties. Eventually, she ran up significant debt and lost her fairy tale home. The alluring image of Rosa in her castle fuels most of the legends and myths.

Upon Rosa's departure, the castle served a variety of uses ranging from a summer camp for boys to house tours. For a brief moment in time during the opening decades of the twenty-first century, it returned to its original purpose as a private cottage residence. Though rooms have been added, with a third floor built onto the back side, the original two floors would be easily recognizable by Rosa today.

# Chapter 2

## BOOMING THE TOWN – The 1880s

It's no surprise that a successful businessman like Samuel Taylor Suit chose Berkeley Springs to build his cottage. It was a chic resort with a booming town. Suit's castle was simply an extravagant example of that boom.

During the 1880s, the rhythm of life in town was a seasonal one and the season was based not on weather but on when visitors came. City neighbors with their own cottages began arriving in May and sometimes stayed as late as November. For the other 400 or so hotel guests, driven by the heat and turmoil of the cities to the pure mountain air, escape and waters of Berkeley Springs, the high season opened when the band arrived at the Berkeley Springs Hotel. From late July through early September, the band played nightly dances including Fancy Dress Balls complete with scores of guests in elaborate costumes. There were also local bands: three coronet bands and one string band according to news reports.

Berkeley Springs in season was dominated by powerful but aging cottagers from Washington and Baltimore, Maryland like Suit. Most seasons during the decade the Grove – as the park area around the springs was called — looked good, cottages were occupied and hotels full. There were picnics of young people at Lovers Leap and private pool parties in the Grove.

Cottages were built and renovated including Suit's notable castle. More and more improvements were made as the decade passed. Street lamps were erected and painted red to hide the defects. Bath Square, as the Grove was also known, was in almost constant development under the efficient management of local bathkeeper Henry Harrison Hunter who began his long reign in 1881. New brick-covered bathhouses, one for women and one for men, replaced antebellum frame ones.

Strolling in The Grove.

Sharing dominance of the economic scene with tourism was First National Tannery owned by the De Fords of Baltimore and operated since before the Civil War. The tannery expanded throughout the decade, employed a couple score of men in town and bought from local providers virtually all the bark the process required. De Ford's plows cleared the streets of snow and he strongly supported bringing the railroad into town. The tannery was embroiled in problems resulting from polluting Warm Springs Run but produced record amounts of leather. Its success was attributed to the spring waters having a peculiar effect in the process of tanning, giving the leather unequalled toughness and durability. During the 1880s, Berkeley Springs was a bustling commercial center with more than 70 enterprises in addition to the tannery and hotels including doctors, painters, carriage and wagon makers, a stage line, blacksmiths, saloons, a photographer and furniture store.

Early in the decade, the telegraph arrived connecting Berkeley Springs with the world. By its close, a railroad spur from the main B&O line along the Potomac River came the six miles to the north end of town. The train made the resort town even more desirable to guests. A train schedule noted that, "By taking #9 you can take dinner at New York City and late supper at this place (Berkeley Springs) or by taking 504 at this place you can have dinner here and supper in New York City." Electricity and public water were soon to arrive.

The railroad spur provided the best tourism season of the decade in 1889 with 500 guests. In September, the *News* printed, "The season at this popular summer resort is about over. The Berkeley Springs Hotel Band has left and the visitors are returning home. This has been one of the gayest and most enjoyable seasons old Berkeley *has seen for many years* and next season, we believe will even exceed it."

# Chapter 3

# THE MAN WHO BUILT THE CASTLE

When people share stories about the castle, they almost always focus on Rosa, the woman for whom it was built. The man who built it remains a shadowy figure. A bit of historical digging shows that Samuel Taylor Suit was remarkably accomplished with a rich history preceding his decision to build a summer cottage that looked like a castle in Berkeley Springs.

Taylor Suit (as he liked to be called) left no evidence of how he first came to know about Berkeley Springs but as a man whose life revolved around his business interests, it's most likely that business brought him here.

Suit was a railroad man and during the 1880s there was a lot of lobbying going on to build a spur into Berkeley Springs from the main B&O line along the Potomac and boom the town. Suit had experience in this specific area. He was also prominent in the world of making whiskey with a long history as a successful distiller. As it happened, one of the prominent summer families at the time were the Crichtons of Baltimore, also in the whiskey business. Railroads and whiskey could have provided both the connections and motivation for Suit to make his way to Berkeley Springs.

The whiskey business came earliest and dominated Suit's career.

Suit was born in Prince Georges County, Maryland, to innkeeper Fielder Suit. Although Taylor Suit escaped his home state while still a teenager, his father never left the area and is buried, alongside his son, at St. Barnabas Cemetery in Oxon Hill, Maryland.

Suit went briefly to Iowa, then settled in Kentucky where he learned the distilling business and eventually married the boss' daughter. An advertising token from 1850 reads, "Kentucky Currency/Salt River/ Bourbon/ ST Suit, distiller" and on the reverse side, "for medicinal use only." Suit was 18 years old. Through his business accomplishments and family connections, young Suit earned the honorary title of Kentucky Colonel.

When he was 23, Suit married Sallie Williams in Louisville. Two years later they had a son, Ebenezer Williams Weller Suit. Sallie died in childbirth along with their son. She was just a week short of her twentieth birthday.

Soon after the deaths of Sallie and his son, Suit turned up in Manhattan where he once again married the daughter of a business connection which increased his wealth, advanced his social position and opened an avenue to acquiring a seat on the New York Stock Exchange.

Taylor Suit and Aurelia Wilmarth were married in 1859. The couple quickly had two children although only Arthur, the son named for Suit's father-in-law, survived.

The elder Arthur Wilmarth was head of Home Life Insurance Company of New York, the first life insurer authorized by the newly founded New York Insurance Department to do business in the state. Merging with Phoenix Mutual Life Insurance Company in 1992, Wilmarth's Home Life is still traded on the New York Stock Exchange as Phoenix Home Life Mutual Insurance Company.

In spite of Suit's Wall Street connections, the 1860 New York Census listed him as a distiller.

There is no record of Samuel Taylor Suit serving on either side of the Civil War. His obituary in the *New York Times* said he came to New York, "where during the war, he became well known as a Wall-street operator. At the close of hostilities he opened the First National Bank of Virginia at Richmond and was its president."

After the war, Suit returned with Aurelia to Maryland and began accumulating real estate, including his 450-acre estate called Suitland as well as parcels connected to his railroad ventures. By 1868, he was firmly entrenched in Maryland.

Suit built a distillery on his Suitland estate. He established orchards growing apples, peaches and cherries that he used in making a range of brandies. The 1870 and 1880 Census has Suit listed as a farmer. Using his own Suitland post office, which also officially established the estate name, Suit developed an impressively successful mail-order liquor business. His company grew and prospered, eventually gaining nationwide sales. He sold his whiskey almost exclusively in brown stoneware jugs

From the private collection of Dennis and Beth Curtin.

of varying sizes and labels. As collectibles today, the little brown jugs are sold for hundreds of dollars. Other containers still found at antique sales are fancy glass decanters bearing the Suit name and Suitland, Maryland.

According to a promotion letter written by Suit in 1882, his whiskey was not sold under a brand name in the contemporary mode. He wrote that he could sell "Pure Old Liquors for private and medicinal purposes." The list specified Old Rye Whiskey, Old Peach Brandy with honey, Old Apple Brandy with rock candy syrup and Old Cherry Brandy.

From 1869 to the time of his death, Suit made his fortune in whiskey, using the money to invest in railroads, agriculture and politics.

His involvement in the world of transportation was complicated and ever-shifting. It began with self-interest. He acquired a permit to build a turnpike road from his estate of Suitland to Washington. Soon after, he moved into railroads.

Postwar America was caught up in railroad fever. The main railroads, especially the B&O, were in place and men like Suit were hustling to build smaller roads that connected the main rails to specific side destinations. There were buy-outs of routes by larger companies and conflicts with dueling railroad companies allowed by the state to lay track in the same area. Suit and his partner and brother-in-law Peter Grimes avoided a shooting war in one of these conflicts in 1873 by working out an agreement with a rival company. Suit kept a section of the disputed route and renamed his railroad the Washington and Chesapeake. Over the next decade he spent about $400,000 – a huge sum in that period – on a pair of other railroad enterprises.

Suit ended his marriage to Aurelia. In 1875, the couple separated and by 1879 their divorce was final. There must have been severe financial consequences since Suit was involved in land and railroad dealings with his father-in-law. For a brief period, Wilmarth even owned the Suitland estate.

The year after the divorce, Suit's impressive frame mansion filled with valuable furniture was destroyed by fire while he was away serving as a judge for agriculture at the Centennial Exposition in Philadelphia. A two-story mansard-roof stable, carriages, harness and several horses were also destroyed. The greatest loss among the horses was his Centennial premium-winning white stallion which he had imported several years earlier from Iceland as breeding stock .

Unfortunately for Suit, officers of the bank had neglected to have insurance policies transferred to the bank so the fire was a serious loss. Suit was forced into bankruptcy and sold the land to pay judgments against him. He never rebuilt the house.

ESTABLISHED 1839.

In    .tion to our full and complete stock of fine Drugs, &c., we have the following celebrated Pure Whiskies for Medicinal purposes:

BOARD OF HEALTH, OFFICE OF THE HEALTH OFFICER, WASHINGTON CITY, D. C., Oct. 1, 1875.

By invitation of Col. S. TAYLOR SUIT, I visited his plantation, SUITLAND, situated in Prince George's County, Maryland, and examined his various brands of liquors, including his "STANDARDS FOR THE DRUG TRADE." I found its strength to be full proof, of fine flavor, and free of all impurities.

FOR MEDICINAL PURPOSES, its reliability as to strength and purity makes it very desirable. Physicians will appreciate how important it is to their success in the treatment of diseases, as well as to the patient, that the stimulants they prescribe should be of a standard and unvarying quality, which desideratum Col. Suit's liquors appear to fill.

P. T. KEENE, M. D,, *Health Officer, District of Columbia.*

BOARD OF HEALTH, WASHINGTON, D. C., August 22, 1875.

*Dear Sir :—*Having tested the quality and strength of S. T. SUIT'S STANDARD WHISKIES OF THE DRUG TRADE, sent me for examination, I have no hesitation in testifying to their  y and fine flavor. I consider them, by virtue of their strength and freedom from all xious qualities, admirably adapted to medicinal uses.

CHRIS. C. COX, M. D., LL. D. *Pres't Board of Health, Washington City, D. C.*

Health Department endorsement

Suit's various business dealings involved him with officials on a national level and before the disastrous fire the mansion at Suitland was the scene of elaborate entertainments. Legends about Suit's parties abound with undocumented claims that both presidents U.S. Grant and James Garfield attended. Particularly notable was a banquet in 1871 attended by friends and various dignitaries including members of the International Joint High Commission meeting in Washington to settle shipping claims from the Civil War. The U.S. Marine Corps Band furnished the music.

As was common in the blazing capitalist culture of the Victorian age in America, businessmen like Suit were in and out of difficult financial straits without it impacting their luxurious way of life. Within three months of declaring bankruptcy, he recovered all his property in Washington, the Suitland estate, Spa Springs Hotel in Blandensburg and continued as president of his railroad, bank and Anacostia Wharf and Docking Company.

During the 1870s, Suit was active in Republican politics. He served for a single term in the Maryland State Senate from 1873 to 1877 with the slogan: "Help me and I will help you." The same year that Suit entered Maryland politics, a pre-teen Rosa Pelham, who would become his third wife, arrived in Washington with her father who had been recently elected to the U.S. Congress from the state of Alabama.

Having sold his Washington City and Point Lookout Railroad to the B&O, by 1883 Suit was enthusiastic over the progress of the Washington and Chesapeake line which had as its end point the resort of Chesapeake Beach, Maryland. He secured rights-of-way and had men working around the clock. The line would bring passengers to the resort in 90 minutes from Baltimore or 45 minutes from Washington. He eventually was elected one of three Commissioners of Chesapeake Beach along with his former estate manager Horace Crosier.

Suit was also involved with a group of men seeking to establish a suburban passenger railroad from downtown Washington to Suitland. Unlike most railroads, this Suburban Street Railway proposed to use horse or other motive power to draw the rail cars, not steam. Apparently, this enterprise was directed to making his Suitland estate more commercially viable since rumors began soon after that he was selling it to the U.S. Department of Agriculture. Currently the land is home for the U.S. Census Bureau.

# Campaign letter from Suit to Thomas Osburn Esq.

Washington City and Point Lookout RR
(Baltimore, Washington & Alexandria branch)
President's office
Washington October 21, 1873

My Dear Sir,

I hope you may get your consent to support me for the Senate. *I know* in my present condition and situation I can be of more benefit to our county and people than Mr. Clark. I am doing all in the power of mortal man to increase the value of our property. All I want is the endorsement of the people and at least my old school mates. If elected I will then have the political power and influence which I do not now possesses. "Help me and I will help you" such was the motto of one of our greatest statesmen and I repeat it to my old friend and school mate, "Help me and I will help you." Help Frank Duvall also.

Your friend, ST Suit

According to his passport application in 1858, Suit was 26 years old, fair in coloring with a Grecian nose. He was not quite 5'8" tall and of medium build. The only foreign trip he was known to have taken was a decade later when he sailed from New York to Le Havre, France aboard the *Ville de Paris*.

DIED

OCTOBER 1, 1888

AGED 56 YEARS

SUIT

Suit is buried among a cluster of family including his sister Kate, father Fiedler and two of his son Arthur's four wives.

It was at this time that Suit began his third family. On September 4, 1883, the 51-year-old successful businessman married Martha Rosa Pelham, 30 years his junior, at her father's home in Washington. As 1886 opened, the recently married Suit began construction on his elaborate cottage in Berkeley Springs. Since his mansion at Suitland had been destroyed by fire before they met and never rebuilt, the couple lived on New Jersey Avenue in Washington.

Suit died on October 1, 1888 of "dropsy of the heart." He is buried at St. Barnabas Church in Oxon Hill, Maryland.

## WHAT HAPPENED TO ARTHUR SUIT?

Arthur B. Suit, born to Taylor and Aurelia in 1862, was known to be an avid sportsman. He raised game chickens and participated in such local events as horse races, cockfights and jousts. He maintained a store, bar and bowling alley on a corner of his father's former estate of Suitland. As sheriff of the small town, Suit built a one-room jail near his house.

The *Washington Post* reported on several cockfights between birds raised by Mr. Suit and various challengers in the early 1890s. A June 1890 match in which Mr. Suit's brown-red Jim Busev beat Matt Allen's Japanese Heavyweight was dubbed "the greatest single shake-bag cock fight that has ever taken place in this country. " Between 100 and 300 spectators were present at the various events and Mr. Suit told the *Post's* sports editor in November of 1891 that he was willing to bet $3,000 – three times the average annual wage at the time – against any challenger. Suitland in the 1890s was also the site of dogfights and annual jousting, or "tilting," tournaments – an earlier version of today's Renaissance Fairs. These tournaments drew 5,000 spectators who also witnessed the crowning of the "Queen of Love and Beauty." In a strange parallel, his stepmother Rosa Suit was attending similar jousting events held by the Crichtons in Berkeley Springs during this same time period.

Arthur married four times and fathered 12 children. His third wife died of ptomaine poisoning on their honeymoon and he then married her younger sister.

# Chapter 4

## THE LAND AND THE BUILDING

The castle reportedly cost $100,000 to build in the late 1880s. The core property is about four acres of ridgetop overlooking the springs, park and town. Its thick stone walls are made of handcut sandstone from nearby Cacapon Mountain carried to the site by horse and wagon. Local families claim members who worked on mining the stone and transporting it to the location while one report allows that 100 German masons did the construction. The castle was not large by mansion standards, only 10,000 square feet and 15 major rooms on two original floors. One historian notes that, shortly before his death, Suit acquired

Taylor and Rosa Suit break ground for their castle

Viewing tower. Built on Fruit Hill Farm in 1880, it was later destroyed by fire after Fourth of July fireworks.

the Oxon Hill Manor Estate and transferred the beautiful old staircase from the manor house to the castle.

The first portrayal of Suit's cottage as a castle appeared in the local *Mercury* newspaper in 1886 when it was described while under construction as "giving one the impression of a handsome castle nestled among the rocks and cliffs of the mountain."

The depiction was repeated again in the April 5, 1888 edition of the Martinsburg *Independent*. "The residence of Mr. S.T. Suit on the side of Warm Springs Ridge is a novelty in this section and strikingly handsome. It is of stone and a regular castle in appearance."

It remained known as the castle.

The land for the castle was part of Fruit Hill Farm. This large tract of land spanned the top of Warm Springs Ridge and extended west to Sir John's Run Road. Colonel John Strother, owner of the Berkeley Springs Hotel, and longtime cottager Edward Pendleton purchased the land in 1856 from the Sherrard family. After a couple of years of temporary owners, Hunter Boyd of Martinsburg bought the tract from the estate of Judge Stewart in 1884, the same year Boyd sold off a piece to Suit. Prior to the sale to Boyd, a hotel was built on the Fruit Hill Farm property. There was also a viewing tower that was a favorite destination for young visitors. Three cottages to rent were opened in 1882. Boyd stated his plans were to complete the hotel and fix up other buildings on the remainder of the land.

In the spring of 1886, Boyd sold the land to a man named Sanders who was identified by the newspaper as being from Boston and who planned "a first class hotel" to open the following year. That same year, 1886, Stewart's observatory on the mountain was reported vandalized.

The St. Elmo Hotel, previously located on the street by the springs, opened at Fruit Hill in 1887 with 80 spacious rooms, fresh spring water in every room, and regular entertainments of euchre parties and musical comedy. Two years later, the manager was selling the hotel's furniture and pieces of the property were sold. It was destroyed by fire in 1890. Eventually, the 750 acres left to Fruit Hill were purchased by Eugene Van Rensselaer who sold it in 1922. Before the final year of the nineteenth century, development was occurring on Fruit Hill Farm land neighboring the castle.

## WHO DESIGNED THE CASTLE?

Fiction and outright fantasy abound when there are no documented facts. Ask any three people the story of how the castle came to be a castle and you will hear that it was drawn on a napkin or a tablecloth; or that Suit himself was an architect and sketched it while seated at the window of the Berkeley Springs Hotel. Variations on the theme of the castle being the bride price for getting the much younger Rosa to marry him are also common.

The name of A.B. Mullett, a famous architect in Washington at the time, is linked to the building in various colorful versions, none documented although it's been suggested he was known to be a visitor to the springs in the 1880s. Legend has Mullett drawing the plan on a menu for his friend Suit saying "here's your castle." As supervising architect for the U.S. Treasury Department, Mullett designed more than 20 fireproof federal buildings across the nation, particularly custom houses, post offices and courthouses. Among his buildings are both the U.S. Treasury and the Old Executive Office Building in Washington. He was known for his monumental Victorian architecture. A popular political target, Mullett was repeatedly investigated for extravagance and once for negligence. He took his own life in 1890.

And then there is Snowden Ashford, an apprentice in Mullett's office, whose work on Berkeley Springs structures is documented. His connection to Berkeley Springs is strengthened by the fact that he married Antoinette Crichton whose family had a major cottage at the springs. However, Ashford was only 19 when Suit broke ground on the castle and did not begin work as a draftsman for Mullett until 1887 casting doubt on the possibility that he designed the castle. It is known that Rosa Suit had Ashford build the gatetower for the castle in 1893. He eventually became Municipal Architect for the city of Washington and, like Mullett, faced official controversy and probes. Among his government designs are the prison at Lorton, Virginia and Eastern High School in Washington.

# Chapter 5

## ROMANTIC ROSA

Without the intriguing Rosa Pelham, Taylor Suit's young wife, prematurely widowed and never to marry again, the stone structure known as Berkeley Castle would not be nearly as alluring.

Rosa was born Martha Rose Pelham in Alabama in 1862. Elected to the U.S. Congress in 1872, her father, Charles Pelham, served only a single term but chose to remain in Washington with his young daughter and practice law. He also worked at the U.S. Treasury Department.

When Rosa and Taylor married on September 4, 1883 in Washington, she was 21 years old. He was 30 years older and had been separated from his second wife for nearly a decade and divorced for four years. There is no documentation of when or where the couple met and courted.

One story suggests that they met at one of Suit's parties at his Maryland mansion in 1879. At that time Suit was described by the *Washington Post* as, "the greatest orchard owner in the neighborhood, whose magnificent fruit farm" at Suitland was full of spring blossoms. He would have been 47 years old and Rosa 18, about the same age as Suit's then-only son Arthur.

By the time the Suits' summer cottage in Berkeley Springs was complete enough for them to take up residence in 1887, the couple had three children: Lula Kate (Louisa), Fielder Pelham and Samuel Taylor Suit.

The local newspaper reported summer cottagers arriving in May 1888 and included the Suits on the list. If they did indeed come to Berkeley Springs, they did not remain long. Suit was reported ill in Washington in June and was dead by the beginning of October.

Rosa arrived in Berkeley Springs in April 1889 following her husband's death. She stayed at the Florence House probably because work was being done to get the castle ready for her residence. Susie Colston

Rosa Pelham Suit

was hired as governess for the children during the months the family spent in Berkeley Springs.

After a brief period of mourning, Rosa made the castle her permanent home and launched what would be almost a decade of glittering parties. Her reputed local beau was Malcolm Crichton, noted horseman and young heir to Ravenswood, another cottage estate in town.

Rosa's comings, goings and parties were a constant in the local newspaper – more so than any other summer resident. Since most of the cottagers in the 1890s were aging, it's no surprise that the young widow who lived in the castle with her three children was doted on by the local press. Her parties were reported in detail and there is no indication that Rosa shunned her celebrity.

The first newspaper report was that a pair of local workmen – supposed to be Robert Roach and Champ Miller – broke the window of the castle and stole two cases of wine, "taking some to Joshua Barney's for a big dance Friday night." The behavior of these men may have motivated Rosa's decision at the end of the season to throw her first big party for the workmen.

The ball was reported by the local press in detail in 1889. "Her beautiful residence was illuminated from base to turret with innumerable Chinese lanterns and the terraces were ablaze with beacon fires. The immense hall was decorated with shields and handsome engravings set in masses of evergreens and fall flowers."

There was dancing to a coronet band and then a march to the supper room at 11:30pm, "for a bountiful repast." The ball closed with a Virginia Reel.

There were evening parties and dance parties, fortune tellers and moonlight excursions on horseback to Lovers Leap. In 1891, an extravagant ball with vanishing musicians was reported by the local press.

"A jolly dance took place at the Castle on Thu night. The musicians arrived promptly and then retired to the front porch to take survey of the surroundings. The moon was in full bloom, she being out there in all her loveliness. They were evidently flirting with the moon before the opera opened, and as they retired suddenly must have lost their way for they did not return. Col. Pendleton was equal to the emergency, procuring an organ and conveying same to the Castle.

"Mrs. Suit was elegantly attired in black crepe with an elegant train that gave her a queenly air. She was untiring in her efforts in order that her guests be well entertained, and made completely at home.

"Not only the elite of our village were invited but all her friends received a cordial invitation to attend the festivities at her feudal home. The supper was simply superb, the punch was of high degree and compounded with care."

By early December, Rosa and family returned to Washington for the winter.

The following season, Rosa's activities even gained mention in the Hagerstown, Maryland newspaper which reported that a driving party on the way to Berkeley Springs from Washington stopped there. Mrs. Suit was named among the party. The paper went on to identify her as the owner of Chesapeake City and mentioned that she was completing the railroad that runs from Washington to that place.

She attended a big Fourth of July celebration in 1892 at the local ballgrounds that included a tournament of "knights on horseback," a favorite sport among the Crichtons and their friends. All the cottage people were there.

By this time, Rosa was living full time in her castle with only occasional brief visits to Washington to attend to business.

In 1893, Rosa had young Washington architect Snowden Ashford design the gatetower now cut off from the main structure by WV 9. Ashford later married Rosa's friend, Antoinette Crichton.

Several parties and balls were held at the castle in 1893. Professor Anton Kasper and his little Bohemian Orchestra, in residence at the Berkeley Springs Hotel for the season, often provided the music.

One event was extensively described in the local press as an old-fashioned country ball attended by about 50 persons, most in evening attire and drawn from those staying at the hotels and cottages in the town. "Quadrilles and cotillions, with an occasional waltz or polka, constituted the programme which was disposed in an admirable manner. The novelty of country dancing made it more enjoyable and the visitors are languid in making it an evening of pleasant recollections."

By 1895, Rosa had water and electricity in the castle. She and the children lived there that winter although monthly trips to Washington were reported.

Rosa continued to throw parties for the next couple of years, but 1895 was the final high season for her. Fireworks were set off from the castle on the Fourth of July; and in late August, there was a major event

Rosa Pelham Suit

at the castle to raise funds to fix Warm Springs Mountain Road. A stage was erected and there were tableaux, music and refreshments.

Financial difficulties and lawsuits were plaguing Rosa. She sold off pieces of Suit's land and in 1898 began renting the castle to satisfy the creditors hounding her, many of whom were local merchants as well as Woodward and Lothrop department store in Washington. About this time, Rosa changed the spelling of her name to Soult as a way of avoiding creditors.

The generally accepted theory is that Rosa partied away her husband's considerable holdings. While she did not seem to exhibit either a thrifty nature or a concern for business, Rosa was also caught in the widespread economic difficulties of the 1890s. From 1893 to 1897, there were two financial panics that caused recession and high unemployment. Several major railroads were bankrupted which may have affected the railroad enterprises Rosa had inherited.

Rosa's financial situation was not the only part of the story that was changing. Berkeley Springs' decline as a premier summer resort and cottage community began with the tragic fires of 1898 and 1901 which destroyed virtually every hotel room in town. Almost overnight, 700 rooms disappeared when first the Berkeley Springs Hotel and then the Fairfax Inn burned.

Rosa and the castle became involved in a scheme to boost Berkeley Springs. It was rumored that millionaire Howard Gould from New York was renting the castle – a claim that was soon exposed by the press as, "an advertising dodge to bring Berkeley into the public eye and to attract attention to several projects looking to Berkeley's development."

## ROSA LOSES THE CASTLE

Although machinations about the castle, its debts and ownership continued for the next couple of years, it was apparent Rosa saw no way to return to her former glamorous life there. She continued to sell off land and furnishings to pay taxes and debts. In 1901 Rosa was getting income from Suitland only by renting 11 acres – scarcely enough to pay taxes. Trustees of her estate advised her to disregard the terms of Suit's will and sell Suitland even though the children were not yet 21. The court agreed and Suitland was sold in 1903.

In 1902 she bought some land on Kesecker's Ford on Sleepy Creek halfway between Berkeley Springs and Hedgesville, West Virginia, and

Castle and gatetower began to deteriorate in the early twentieth century.

built a cottage. Today, this is where WV9 crosses Sleepy Creek. The newspaper described it as a beautiful cottage on a romantic spot crowing that she and her children were leading a thoroughly idyllic life. Private recollections describe it as not substantial but more the construction of a summer place with unfinished floors and unplastered walls. The family spent a couple of years moving between there and the castle.

Tragedy struck Rosa in 1905 when her 21-year-old daughter Louisa died of typhoid fever in Berkeley Springs. Published recollections from neighbors at the time all agreed that Rosa and her daughter had a difficult relationship. The local newspaper had a tribute to Louisa who had continued to use the Suit spelling. She was in training as a nurse and was in Morgan County when a doctor convinced her to take care of his patient who had typhoid. She went to the home of Lunger Michael to nurse the patient, caught the disease and died there. Louisa is buried in Bethel Church graveyard near Sleepy Creek Village.

Castle overlooking town circa 1910

For the next decade, ownership of the castle became a complicated affair with several auction sales and indications that Rosa inherited some money, possibly from her father, and moved back. Owners included Rosa's two sons as well as the Bank of Morgan County. It was not until 1923 that local businessman George Cunningham bought the castle with a clear deed.

Once she was finally evicted from the castle, Rosa continued to live in Morgan County in a series of rundown rental houses in Timber Ridge District including one in Oakland and one in Greenwood. She remained there until her son Samuel moved her to St. Louis, Missouri, in 1935. By the following year, she was living in Coeur d'Alene, Idaho with her son Fiedler who also used the Soult spelling.

Many stories are told by local folks over the years about their encounters with Rosa while she continued to live in Morgan County. Rosa smoked, a scandalous activity for a woman at the time. Local historian Fred Newbraugh would tell the story of how the Hotel Dunn would order her gold-tipped Malachrino Cigarettes especially made for ladies.

Letters dated 1936 indicated Fiedler was unhappy having his mother in Idaho. He asked about the disposition of the castle and other property, felt he and his brother had been deprived of their inheritance and wanted to know if Rosa returned to Morgan County would the county take care of her. Fiedler claimed he left home when he was 21, and his brother left at 16. More than a decade later, Rosa died in Coeur d'Alene. The name on her death certificate was Rosa Pelham Soult.

# THE SAMUEL TAYLOR SUIT WILL
## January 1888

Samuel Taylor Suit's will is readily available in both the Morgan County Courthouse and in Washington.

In his will, completed in January 1888, Suit identifies himself as a resident of Washington. He makes several minor bequests to family including $2500 to his first son, Arthur, and $500 to his sister Marian. He does not mention his other sister Kate who was married to his longtime business partner Peter Grimes. He does give his nephew S. Taylor Grimes $500. His nieces and nephews, unspecified in name or number, receive $250 each. He also left Saint Barnabas Church, where he was eventually buried, $500 "for the benefit of said Church grounds."

Suit gave the remainder of his estate to Rosa and their three children: Lula Kate, Fielder Pelham and Samuel Taylor Suit "share and share alike." The shares were to be held in trust for the children. They would receive half at 21 and the other half at 26. He appointed Rosa as trustee for the estate unless she remarried, in which case the trusteeship would be handed to two men: William A. and J. Holdsworth Gordon. Suit gave the trustees, whether Rosa or the two men, authority to sell everything in the estate except for Suitland and "my Berkeley Springs property;" both of which were to be held for the use of Rosa and the children.

There are no records indicating that Rosa brought any dowry to the marriage but in the will, Suit states that her shares in the estate be accepted "in lieu of dower."

The three witnesses to the will appeared in a Washington court within two weeks of Suit's death to attest that Suit did indeed sign this document in their presence.

What this will does not do, contrary to many stories, is require Rosa to finish building the castle in order to get the rest of the estate. The provision that she remains trustee for the children, and therefore in control of the estate, only if she does not remarry, provides motivation for the fact that this wealthy young widow never did take another husband.

# Chapter 6

## VICTORIAN BERKELEY SPRINGS
### The 1890s Boom & Bust

While the 1880s were the decade that explained Taylor Suit and how he ended up in Berkeley Springs building a castle, the 1890s were the decade of Rosa and how she lost it.

The final decade of the nineteenth century dawned with great promise in the fashionable spa town of Berkeley Springs. Thanks to a rare alliance of tanneries and hotels, a spur of the railroad had been brought into town two years earlier. There were almost 1000 hotel rooms, including the Berkeley Springs Hotel on the south end of the Grove and the St. Charles (Fairfax Inn) sprawling along Fairfax Street at the north

Berkeley Springs Hotel artwork

end. The St. Charles stretched into the block west to Warm Springs Run. Nearby Washington St. was covered with the buildings of De Ford's Tannery as were several other blocks.

More than a dozen elaborate cottages brought their high-society owners to town during the season which for hotel guests traditionally reached its peak in July and August. The cottagers usually stayed longer, extending the season from April through November. Big parties were anticipated entertainment.

In residence at his Glen Luta estate, Eugene Van Rensselaer invested heavily in Berkeley Springs, bringing both public water and electricity to town. It would be justifiable to call 1894 the year of the Van Rensselaers. He staged a huge celebration to launch the bringing of electric lights to Berkeley Springs. Mrs. Van Rensselaer was a force in the Village Improvement Association which staged theatrics and bazaars to raise money for beautification. That year, the group gave a public fountain for the Grove. A reservoir was built atop the mountain as part of the water works. Touting the establishment of both public water and electricity, the B&O magazine crowed that "persons seeking a home in a prosperous town and county should look over Berkeley Springs before locating elsewhere," calling it one of the progressive towns, county seats and health resorts of the south.

Tennis was the popular game as well as horse sports glamorized by the Crichtons who built Ravenswood, their estate on Johnson's Mill Road, as the decade opened. The facade of society season and cottage fun persisted through the 1890s although there was steady decline beneath the surface. In 1890, the B&O Railroad had a summer schedule particularly to serve the springs. The train helped swell the number of people attending the 1891 Fourth of July celebration to 5000. The crowds enjoyed a parade, ox roast and tournament with nine knights on horseback including three young Crichtons.

A year-'round business community emerged in this decade. *The News* reported, "It is the comment of every visitor that Berkeley Springs is improving as fast as any town in the state." Twenty-five new buildings were going up or getting a first coat of paint as the decade began including stores, cottages and the new Methodist Church. More expansion was planned and undertaken. By the end of the 1890s, the buzz was all about tomato canneries springing up throughout the county.

Both major industries – tanning and hotel – suffered severe losses through the decade. In 1890, leather manufactured at the De Ford Tannery in Berkeley Springs took first place at the World's Exposition in New Orleans. At the same time, De Ford lost court battles for polluting Warm Springs Run and the Potomac River. By decade end, the newspaper reported, "Beauty of Potomac gone... it looks like a vast tannery vat in motion – both at Paw Paw and the run from Berkeley Springs." Pollution was so severe, the B&O stopped using Potomac River water in its tanks. A literal death blow for the tannery came in 1897 when De Ford died and a U.S. Senate vote put duties on hides.

Henry Harrison Hunter retired in 1894 after more than a decade as bathkeeper at the Grove leaving more time for his inventing and mining. As a result of Hunter's prospecting, the sandworks started and within a generation was dominating the local economy, regularly employing a large number of hands. While no one at the time linked Hunter's leaving with a rise of turmoil and disputes over leasing the springs to private interests, the two coincided. The springs and surrounding park area suffered by mid-decade, having received no improvements in years. Calls for straightening, deepening and clearing Warm Springs Run increased by late 1897 when heavy October rains flooded the town doing great damage to many buildings. *The News* continued its support for leasing the springs citing disastrous seasons for visitors and a reputation for bad hotels, worse bathing facilities and lurking diseases.

## THE CRICHTON FAMILY

The Crichtons of Baltimore were typical of the new segment of the cottage community that dominated the Berkeley Springs season in Victorian times. They did not have century-long roots the way the Pendletons did. They were not as prominent as Judge William Dole, Abraham Lincoln's Commissioner of Indian Affairs. They were not community investors like the Van Rensselaers.

For our purposes, they are far more important because of their connection to the Suits in several ways – some speculative, some documented.

Like other cottagers, the Crichtons initially rented a place for their seasonal stays. The father, Malcolm, was in the liquor business and almost certainly knew the successful distiller Taylor Suit. Malcolm Sr. died in 1891 two years after he built Ravenswood, an estate and house just on the outskirts of town. The year after the old man's death, local builder J.W. Hunter constructed an addition to the house. It was the largest of the cottages at the time.

By 1908, Ravenswood was being used as a boarding house and was eventually torn down in 1931. Today, what was the estate property holds dozens of houses extending from Johnson's Mill Road over the hillside and down to WV9 just east of its intersection with US522.

At the time Crichton acquired the estate, it bordered Glen Luta, owned by Eugene Van Rensselaer. Originally built in 1872 and renovated in 1886, Glen Luta covered most of the area that is today the southeast corner of WV9 and US522.

The Crichtons had five children and were involved with horses, another interest shared with Taylor Suit. In 1891, they competed as "knights" in a local tournament. The three boys were 18, 16 and 11 respectively.

The eldest son, Malcolm Jr. was repeatedly linked romantically with the widowed Rosa during her partying years of the 1890s. The stories of a romance are unsubstantiated and suspect since Rosa was nearly a decade older. The local newspaper only mentioned Rosa and the Crichtons as companions in group events including a moonlight ride and parties at Ravenswood.

One interesting comment in the paper states that in 1890 Rosa had an accident with her horse and then goes on to say that Malcolm Crichton Jr. or relatives have repeated accidents with their horses who seem either very high strung or the Crichtons are incompetent. By 1893, the newspaper carried a big front page ad by Malcolm Crichton listing horses for the season including service fees. The Morgan County Census of 1900 records Malcolm's occupation as manager of a stock farm. It also indicates three servants living at Ravenswood.

The oldest Crichton daughter, Antoinette, was closer in age to Rosa and eventually married Washington architect Snowden Ashford. A decade before they married, Ashford was hired to design an addition to Ravenswood and the gatetower at the castle.

# Chapter 7

## THE CASTLE AFTER ROSA

The twentieth century saw the castle used for a haphazard series of commercial purposes from tea room and artist retreat to site of a boys' camp. Improved transportation created a state highway heading west from downtown Berkeley Springs in 1924. It cut through castle grounds marooning the gatetower on the opposite side of the highway. Previously, folks headed west from town used today's Cornelius Ave.

Auction sales of the castle were announced more than once and in 1916 it was sold to the Bank of Morgan County. After being offered and withdrawn from sale several times in 1923, local businessman George Cunningham finally bought it, moved his family there and owned the castle through 1938 bringing some stability.

Rosa did not give up her castle easily. Soon after Cunningham bought the property from the bank, he was suing Rosa. He claimed Rosa was detaining or withholding the property. She had a room with her furniture in it. Rosa said she had a contract with the bank deriving from a 1913 lawsuit stipulating that if she surrendered all claims to the property she could occupy and use the north end for the rest of her life as a "place to erect and use a small building as a tea room for her support and maintenance without exacting any charge for the use." She maintained that this fact was known to Cunningham at the time he purchased the property from the bank. Since she was not allowed to build the space and establish the tea room, there was no place for her to move her possessions from a room in the castle. The jury found in Cunningham's favor.

Initially, Cunningham gave up his lease on the Dunn Hotel in town and claimed he would operate the castle as a hotel once it was expanded. Other than a brief stint as a lodging place in 1932 operated by Ward Yost, there is no indication Cunningham's plan ever happened. Instead, the castle became the site of a variety of uses including Pastime Club

In a Letter to the Editor, a woman said she visited in 1929: "We found the place deserted, the house in ruins and the property overgrown with briars and weeds..."

dances in 1924, a shop and retreat for artists and writers in 1929 and Friday night dances at The Old Castle Club in 1936.

The castle seemed to draw dreamers who promised uses for it that never materialized. One of those was Bertha Taylor Voorhorst who was described by the local press as a nationally-known writer. In 1929, she leased the castle with an option to buy and joined with Cunningham's daughter Kathleen to run a retreat for artists and writers. Kathleen was also to run a tea room and antique shop there. In May of that year, the pair had an opening reception for the public with a lecture on floriculture. Voorhorst also planned to use it as a summer home. Ultimately, she never bought the property.

What really happened over the next decade were local dances, weddings, parties and tours. A new state road map in 1934 had a photo of the castle identifying it as the Berkeley Castle Club.

In 1935, it was reported that 35 people, or more, were touring the castle each day. When Mrs. Voorhorst opened the castle that summer, the newspaper noted that "Louise Bond, occupant of castle, was prepared to

Tomato Festival princesses

give efficient service to invalids or any in need of special care or a physician in charge."

February 1936 was a notable month with a special Valentine's celebration and a Colonial Ball at the end of the month that featured a parade, speeches and a re-enactment of George Washington receiving the flag from Betsy Ross.

In April of 1937, the castle was once again offered at a tax sale although there is no indication that it was purchased. In September, it was the location for the Queen's Ball at the first Tomato Festival.

## MONTE VITA – A RANCH CAMP FOR BOYS

One of the most intriguing uses of the castle occurred during the late 1930s and 1940s. Dr. Ward Kesecker purchased it in 1938 from Cunningham, leased neighboring acreage and established Monte Vita which he called a ranch camp for boys. He advertised it as "a bit of New England transplanted to the Alleghenies plus mineral waters from famous springs."

Kesecker was an educator with a law degree as well as his PhD in education. His board of directors was drawn mostly from his connections in Washington but also included two local residents: Morgan County school superintendent Price Clark and local physician Dr. E.H.Willard.

According to Kesecker, the camp included either 300 or 500 acres of land and used the castle as its base. There were stables and a riding tournament with jousting poles that must have summoned the ghosts of the Crichtons. The boys were allowed access to the mineral pools in the park which "add pep and vigor." They swam in Cacapon Lake and took overnight boat trips down the Cacapon River to the Potomac and then to Hancock, Maryland. On the boat trips, they would camp at Sir John's Run where the first steamboat had been developed by James Rumsey. Accommodations for overnight guests were offered in the castle.

Kesecker claimed that when he bought the castle, it was a "desolate ruin inhabited by spiders, bats. etc." He made physical changes to the castle including a new roof. An addition to the back of the castle provided a third floor living area although of far inferior construction to the original stone structure. Mr. and Mrs. Ward Yost returned as caretakers.

In May 1938, a Folk Festival was scheduled at the castle. It was planned as an annual affair to be presented by the Evergreen 4-H Club.

Monte Vita booklet cover

*Monte-Vita*

Monte Vita boys on roof

Activities included square dancing, cowboy songs and stunts and Swedish, Dutch and Irish folk dances in costumes. Folk singing and fiddle tunes were provided by the Morgan County Ridge Runners under the leadership of E. Hovermale.

In 1939, Kesecker made the castle available for the two-week Potomac Valley Antique and Hobby Fair. Prizes were given in numerous categories including quilts, snuff boxes, glassware, dolls, vases, parasols, matchcovers and dozens more. "The Castle has taken on the appearance of a well-stocked museum," reported one newspaper. Mary Dyche Hunter's collection of 300 dolls won first prize.

Kesecker spun many fanciful tales about the castle to various news and magazine writers. He also conducted public tours inaugurating what became a tradition of embroidering or outright making up stories.

Kesecker's general narrative about the castle was almost a total fabrication. He identified Suit as an architect and referred to him as Soult, an altered spelling Taylor Suit never used; it was Rosa's invention. Kesecker claimed Suit sketched plans on a napkin for his sweetheart as they sat in Berkeley Springs. He exaggerated the age difference saying Suit was past 60, Rosa was 17. As Kesecker's fairy tale continued, he said Taylor and Rosa climbed the mountain, marked out boundaries and bought the mountainside. A few days later they were married. Many of his fancies live on today in stories people and publications tell about the castle.

1960s postcards of the castle exterior and interior rooms.

Various people lived at the castle as everything from caretakers to renters until Walter Bird purchased it from Kesecker in 1954.

## TOURISM ATTRACTION AND HOUSE TOURS

For nearly 50 years, Walter Bird conducted multiple house tours daily and spun tall tales about the castle's history to thousands of visitors each year. Countless people today remember tours they took as children. Eventually it was placed on the National Register of Historic Places.

Bird and his tour guides said that among sights in the castle was an "iron gate from a duel ground," and that "the English ivy that covers the south end of the castle was reportedly brought from the home of Shakespeare, Stratford on Avon, England." They told of secret tunnels, a dungeon, ghosts and a history of murders that previously were unknown.

In fact, there is a dungeon of sorts with access through the first floor catering kitchen. Stairs curve down an opening made by blasting through the rough, natural rock of the mountainside which makes up the exterior wall of the space. The tunnel supposedly led from the castle basement to the gatetower built by Rosa in 1893 and reportedly

Photo courtesy Hermann Esser

Underground "dungeon."

collapsed during road construction in the 1920s. Searches for tunnels by local folks 100 years later turned up none.

Highpoints in the castle's half-a-century history as a tourist attraction included an April 1976 public reception for the Mayor of Bath, England, Miss Cicely Edmunds staged by the Town of Bath Bicentennial Commission.

In the final years of the 1980s, local innkeeper Sandy Kauffman was the exclusive caterer for the castle, managing weddings and other events. The local New World Theater Company worked with Kauffman

Jill Klein Rone portrayed Rosa Suit in the murder mystery as well as later holiday teas for the Museum of the Berkeley Springs.

and staged an elaborate and original murder mystery based on the castle's history. From this grew a proposal for a Castle Foundation that envisioned an amphitheater, restaurant and video broadcast studio. The group proposing this staged a street theater version of storming the castle on Bastille Day 1990.

One of the most fanciful of plans for the castle came in 1991-92 when longtime owner Walter Bird partnered with Clifford Queen. Along with local magician and actor Rodney Pittman, the pair spun a remarkable story of $10 million in planned renovations including a 40-car parking lot and room for three buses. According to the plans, parking was needed for the future hotel that would be built on the mountainside in the shape of a

Rosa's portrait in bedroom

Photo courtesy Hermann Esser

3rd floor deteriorated.

castle. Folks would be driven to this hotel in a chariot. They also had plans for a medieval museum behind the castle. A proposed opening in the summer of 1992 for a 140-seat restaurant and dining on the rooftop never materialized. What did occur was a slow but steady deterioration of the castle through the end of the decade.

## GHOSTBUSTERS

Unsubstantiated rumors that the castle was haunted gained credence with the auction sale in 2000 when one member of a group of Leesburg, Virginia investors which bought the castle went rogue and announced to the press that they were planning to establish an institute for the study of paranormal activity – a type of ghostbuster college – based on claims of "electromagnetic anomalies." Within two weeks, both the idea and the investor disappeared, perhaps because there were no ghosts there. Prior to the auction sale, the Virginia Scientific Research ghost investigators claimed they detected paranormal activity pinpointing Rosa's bedroom and the drawing room. They saw no apparitions.

The auction house catalogue for the sale listed more than 300 specific items and then stated that all remaining uncataloged items would be sold afterwards. Specific items ranged from glassware, china, and tapestries to a three-piece parlor suite and dozens of other pieces of furniture. None were identified as original to the castle.

The remaining investors, Hermann Esser and Frank Bredimus, nearly doubled the purchase price with their repairs and renovations which included rewiring, installing functioning kitchens, a new roof and repointing the stone exterior. Lots of work was needed since the Bird regime did little to maintain the physical structure – especially the third floor living area addition which appeared ready to fall down. The investment group floated a variety of ideas that never took root, then offered it for sale at auction again in 2002.

## ANDREW GOSLINE

Enter Andrew Gosline, a central-casting vision of a castle owner.

"I try to do different things on my birthday," said Gosline. "I read an article in the *Wall Street Journal* about a castle for sale in West Virginia. I was surprised. A castle in West Virginia? I came to Berkeley Springs, a place I'd never heard of, to see it." A month later Gosline returned for the auction with his two sons. He never planned to buy the property

Great Hall

Dining Room

Gargoyles

but got caught up in the bidding. "My oldest son turned to me and said 'Dad, I think you just bought a castle'."

Rosa Pelham Suit would have approved of Andrew Gosline owning her precious stone cottage known to the world as Berkeley Castle, especially since he hung her portrait in his suite. He enhanced the gardens, expanded the terraces, added a waterfall and rebuilt the turret gatetower. The three-story tower, battlements and exterior walls of local sandstone on the main castle building received additional work and century-old mortar was replaced. Rosa's bedroom and the adjacent childrens' rooms became Gosline's three-room suite and the wood-paneled library was transformed into a game room. Calculating the numbers, there are eight fireplaces, 16 rooms, nine full bathrooms and three halves as well as a kitchen on every floor.

With Gosline's purchase, twenty-first century Berkeley Castle was returned to its original nineteenth century purpose as a private home, causing endless sighs and moans of dismay from visitors who remembered it open for house tours. Gosline opened the castle for public use for weddings, photo shoots and rare community events like the annual Holiday Tea for the Museum of the Berkeley Springs.

The gargoyles which crouch on parapets and battlements are not original to the castle. Gosline added them because he liked them. As for ghosts, Gosline stated that "Rosa's never joined me in the suite."

In a strange twist of the legend, Gosline, like Suit, married a young beauty and soon after suffered a heart attack but, this being the twenty-first century, modern medicine kept him alive. His bride left and he continued to live in the castle until his death in November 2014.

# Chapter 8

## MYSTERIES, BASELESS LEGENDS AND UNSUBSTANTIATED RECOLLECTIONS
Is It Haunted?

### ALL SPIRITS ARE NOT THE SAME.

Susan Sheppard is a famed psychic who leads authentic ghost tours in Parkersburg, West Virginia, rated among the top 10 in the country. She explains that seeing a ghost is quite rare. Most hauntings are experienced in other ways, through smells, moving or disappearing objects, sounds, doors opening or closing, cold spots and electrical malfunctions. They show up in different areas of the building or place, and appear to people in different ways.

There are a variety of spirits.

Energy imprints are like a recording of a tragic or dramatic event. They are not earth-bound spirits and have no consciousness. Although they can look very solid and real, they cannot see or interact with you. These are the most common of "hauntings."

Intelligent spirits are spirits or souls who remain attached to something they left behind on earth. They move about as they wish and are seldom stuck here or earth bound. Circumstances, such as unfinished business, will draw them back to interact with the living.

Poltergeists are sporadic bursts of psychic activity where objects are tossed or moved. They are often mischievous.

Non-human entities are called Djinn, fairies, angels or demons. They have never lived as people but will sometimes project themselves to be human.

Shadow people ghosts are also non-human and appear only as a dark shadow with no real features. They are attached to certain areas and tend not to travel from that spot very much.

Spirit manifestations feed upon emotions such as fear, anger and sometimes even happiness.

There are bona fide mysteries associated with the Berkeley Castle. How did Taylor and Rosa meet? What brought them to Berkeley Springs? And what was the source for the concept and design of the castle?

These few mysteries pale in comparison to the seemingly endless supply of baseless legends. Rosa Suit could bear personal responsibility for some of the misinformation. Local historian Fred Newbraugh would tell the story of accompanying Mrs. Voorhorst, who was renting the castle, and another individual to visit and interview Rosa one day in the early 1930s. Mrs. Voorhorst's guest kept trying to get Rosa to confirm the stories she'd heard. When asked whether the drawing for the castle was on a napkin, menu or tablecloth, Rosa shrugged and answered: "which do you like best?"

Subsequent owners of Rosa's castle took her at her word and either embroidered facts or fabricated details completely. When the press came in contact with fabrications they simply reported them as facts. Magazine writers would lift errors from a previous story and pass them on as fact. The "official" Berkeley Castle brochure of the mid-1950s contributed greatly to spreading misinformation.

One prevalent body of misinformation had to do with who Taylor Suit and Rosa were.

One source claimed that Taylor Suit served as Ambassador to England under presidents Grant and Hayes. In fact, during the administrations of those two presidents there were five ambassadors including the noted romantic poet James Russell Lowell. Samuel Taylor Suit was not among the five.

- One woman claimed Rosa was her Sunday school teacher in Washington. They stayed acquainted because her parents had a cottage in Berkeley Springs. She said that the courtship of Taylor Suit and Rosa Pelham sparked scandal as he divorced his wife. The church made Rosa resign from teaching the children. The facts that can be proven are that Suit and his second wife were separated in 1875 when Rosa was no more than 14 years old. Technically, the divorce was not final until 1879.

- One of the more outrageous stories has several variations including one in which two of Rosa's purported beaux were thrown to their deaths off the roof of the castle. In reading all the newspaper reports of Rosa's doings, there is no reason to believe that she was either capable of such a crime or that it would go unreported in the local press if not blazoned across headlines in the national papers.

There was some mention in the local press in June 1893 but it was built around reports of a ghost and then ascribed to legend. The claim was that there were ghosts at the castle including Rosa (who was still alive), the Colonel (Suit), a beau of Rosa's named Jawbone and a little girl of seven. "Legend has it that two of Rosa's suitors died under mysterious circumstances. It is rumored that Rosa, in a fit of rage threw Jawbone off a balcony and that she may have caused the death of a second when she speared him with an umbrella."

A century or so later, it's hard to know the factual base for a story like this. There were two incidents that may have contributed. In May 1890, Rosa's fine driving horse was left hitched to the cart in the charge of a small boy. The newspaper reported: "Somehow the horse backed over the wall and fell many feet and died. Mrs. Suit was especially fond of the animal."

Earlier that year, it was noted that Rosa was advertising to sell a pair of mules.

Two years later, it was reported that, "Mrs. Rosa P. Suit narrowly escaped what might have been a fatal accident. One of her horses attached to a vehicle backed over the terrace at the Castle and how the occupants escaped serious injury is a mystery but fortunately no one was badly hurt."

England's BERKELEY CASTLE

- Thanks to the internet it's easy to disprove the claim that Berkeley Castle is a half-scale replica of the famed Berkeley Castle in Berkeley, England. At best, it's about a fifth the size and does not appear to be a replica of anything. Is it the only English Norman castle in the United States? Maybe. Nearly 100 "castles" in the U.S. are listed and there may be more that never made anyone's list. None represents itself as English Norman (or Romanesque) although there is one in New England with similar architecture to ours in Berkeley Springs.

- The fact that Suit became an honorary Kentucky Colonel during his time in that state, probably awarded because of his business activities, seems to have confused many journalists as well as the tour guides looking for a good angle. He is mentioned in various articles as being a soldier in the Union army as well as one in the Confederate ranks. One enterprising writer took his alleged southern involvement one step further claiming that Suit "fought with Robert E. Lee." Facts are that Samuel Taylor Suit is not listed on the National Park Service roster in either army. Other documented evidence indicates that he sat out the Civil War on Wall Street making money.

- A local writer during the 1930s, Mary Hunter (later Swartz), may have invented more tales about the castle and its inhabitants than even the tour guides. She was one of the earliest sources of fabricated and erroneous material, writing at about the same time that Rosa Suit was finally leaving Morgan County.

  Her false claims about Samuel Taylor Suit began with his physical description. According to Mary, he was "a large man, in fact almost powerful." His passport description claims him to be not quite 5'8" and of medium build. She refers to him as Judge Soult, a reference no one else ever made. Although Rosa altered the spelling of the name, reportedly to avoid creditors after his death, Suit never did. There are other unsubstantiated claims about both Taylor and Rosa being well-educated, and that they came to Berkeley Springs so their ailing daughter Louisa, born in 1884, could take the waters. She adds the infant to the list, along with Rosa, of those to whom Suit promised to build a castle. Mary Hunter credits Snowden Ashford with building the castle "as he did many other structures in Bath in that era" in spite of his being only 19 when construction started. There is no indication that Ashford ever built anything except the castle gatetower and addition to Ravenswood.

  Hunter makes a claim about a Bismark Crichton (which she misspells) whose education as a physician Rosa allegedly paid for and then was abandoned by him. Crichton family records do not support this, showing four sons: Arthur, Malcolm, McPherson and James. McPherson was an M.D. lovingly referred to as "Uncle Doctor." Family records report he was legendary for driving like a mad man and had five wives none of them Rosa. She also claims the Suits kept a stable of racing horses; however it was the Crichtons who trained and kept horses in Berkeley Springs.

- Local historian Fred Newbraugh wrote occasionally about the castle and most of his statements were well-documented including numerous interviews with Rosa and people who knew her. No secret tunnels appear in Newbraugh's writings. One alluring story was told to Newbraugh in the 1950s by the son of Kaspar, the famed bandleader who played often at the Berkeley Springs Hotel. After a big ball at the hotel, Rosa had the Kasper band come to the castle to play until sunrise. Young Kaspar said they expected friends of Rosa's would be invited but they were not. "We played the whole night through for the hostess and her lover." The purported lover was not identified.

## MISINFORMATION IN PRINT

• The *Baltimore Sun* published one of the first journalistic reports of castle legend portrayed as fact. It was 1950 and the journalist George Kahne interviewed owner Ward Kesecker featuring his house tours.

Based on Kesecker's information, the article said Rosa was destitute and left the castle which stood abandoned for half a century. This version identified two secret entrances to the tunnel and dungeon in the ballroom, including one under the staircase. The not-secret entrance to the cellar/dungeon and tunnel through the kitchen was reportedly blocked because it was unsafe. The article claimed that the tunnel ran under the grounds to the gatetower although no reason for such an elaborate construction was given. As an explanation, Kesecker offered the legend of a coachman and kitchen maid, secret meetings and an elopement through the tunnel. Mrs. Kesecker had "weird story duty." She described the ghost "Jawbones" who haunted the library and the ballroom and hid behind an unopened door on the second floor at the end of the hallway.

Kahne also said Rosa always flew her private flag from the turret of what he called a copy of a 13th century Norman castle. Kahne made the common mistake of claiming George Washington surveyed the town. In castle lore, he cited the non-existent sections of the will stating that Rosa had to finish the castle to get Suit's money. The article stated that Kesecker converted to other uses a Roman bath as well as the legendary wine cellar and dungeon.

• One of owner Walter Bird's successful efforts was to market the castle for tours. There were billboards and brochures everywhere in the region. An early 1950s brochure was so laden with hyperbole that it's hard to cut through it. The brochure refers to the castle as "a bit of the historic Rhine of Medieval times transported to new America." It is likened to "the Castle of Enchantment referred to by a great English writer."

The brochure's story of the castle also was rife with twisted facts traceable to Ward Kesecker and it probably served as the basis for various erroneous articles later. "According to legend, " the brochure read, "many years ago a wealthy architect, seated by a window in a Berkeley Springs Hotel, told his young sweetheart that if she would marry him, he would build her a castle on the mountain overlooking the town. As she talked, he sketched the plans on her handkerchief. The 17-year-old girl accepted his proposal. He was past 60. The next morning they climbed the mountainside and he designated by cane the exact corners of the castle and proceeded to buy the mountainside. They were married a few days afterwards and divided their time between Washington and Berkeley Springs during the next six years while the Castle was being built."

- In 1970, Morris Fraden wrote about the castle for *Valley of History* magazine. Fraden had a mixture of facts – mostly from Newbraugh – and pure fantasy including stories of ghosts and elopements told at the summer camp. As many others who mistakenly reported about Taylor Suit's will, Fraden claimed it required Rosa to complete the castle.

- Ted Shelsby did an extensive article for the *Baltimore Sun* magazine in 1972. Shelsby used few documented facts and lots of legends. He had Suit at 65 when he married a 17-year-old Rosa in Berkeley Springs. The author claimed Suit drew the castle, climbed the mountain then bought the land. Rosa and Suit were married in a few days. Blocks of granite from Cacapon Mountain were reportedly used to build the castle. The mountain is actually sandstone. The article reported that when Rosa died, she was buried by the county. In fact, she died in Idaho.

  And then there were the tunnel rumors. Like Kahne, Shelsby located an entrance to the dungeon and secret tunnel in the ballroom that for safety reasons was blocked off. The story claimed the tunnel was built so Rosa's coachman could secretly visit his kitchen maid girlfriend whose father, the head gardener, disapproved. They eloped through the tunnel. As for ghosts, he said there was a ghost in the paneled library on the second floor in spite of tour guides of the time saying there were no ghosts. And for monsters, he quoted from a batch of papers written by fifth graders in 1958.

- In 1979, an article released by West Virginia Tourism claimed Suit "served under Robert E. Lee." It also described nightlife never before mentioned in local history:

  "When the casino in town closed for the night, the guests would adjourn to the castle to continue their games of chance."

- Even the description on the U.S. Census Bureau's website has misinformation. They repeated the false claim that Suit's will stipulated that his young widow had to complete the project before she could inherit his fortune.

- A typed manuscript for *Berkeley News* from Roy, John and Frank Kesecker had too many errors to list them all. They claimed Taylor Suit was an Englishman, a general and one of the outstanding architects in Washington, and that he promised he would build Rosa a "castle in the air." They described the castle as having 55 rooms and a panel beside one of the fireplaces in the great hall that opened at the touch of a finger to a secret passageway.

- A G.M. Farley article, possibly for *West Virginia Magazine*, presented much of the story accurately. He wrote that caretaker Ruth Bishop denied knowledge of ghosts, ghouls, dungeons and secret passageways. Most of the Suit biographical information was correct until he cited legends that have Suit as a French officer or a German architect and Rosa a German princess. He gave inaccurate historic background of Berkeley Springs which he claimed became the name of the town about 1863. In fact, the formation of Berkeley County in 1772 initiated use of the name which was made the official postal name in 1802. The misinformation continued with claims that Mullett designed, and Snowden Ashford was hired to build, the castle. Further, he repeated the lore that English ivy on the castle was from Shakespeare's home.

- *Berkeley Springs – Where the Elite of the East Met to Frolic All Night… and Recover All Day* offered a string of misinformation about Indians and early history including that George Washington discovered the springs. In fact, when a 16-year-old Washington first encountered the springs on a surveying trip, he called them "ye fam'd warm springs." The article cited Washington Irving and Mark Twain as great writers who did their work at the springs. There is no indication Mark Twain ever set foot in Berkeley Springs but Irving did come visit his friend John Pendleton Kennedy who summered regularly at the springs.

The castle fiction is standard. Suit and Rosa were 65 and 18. Rosa's father was identified as a jurist from Kentucky. In this version, an architect scribbled the design on a menu causing Rosa to relent after having rejected Suit many times. There were lavish gardens and vineyards as well as a secret tunnel. More original misinformation stated that Rosa lost her money and lived in rags. She had a shrill voice and people thought her a witch. Her son eventually took her to his home in Colorado.

## UNSUBSTANTIATED REMEMBRANCES

• A 1978 interview with former castle caretaker Amma Catlett relayed several interesting, although unsubstantiated, anecdotes about Rosa. Catlett claimed that during Rosa's castle days, a platform was built on the south terrace, opening from the ballroom. Pine torches and Japanese lanterns gave light for dancing. Rosa gave many parties for the children of the community and also the boys from Old Dominion Academy which her sons attended. (ODA opened in Berkeley Springs in 1914.) The students had the use of the castle's second floor library. At Halloween parties for children, Rosa filled an old glove with wet sand and took the children to the tunnel where they "shook" hands with the glove and played other scary games.

According to Catlett, Rosa made jelly in three-color layers in jelly glasses and sold it at the castle during the lean days when she opened the castle to visitors. After the loss of the castle, she moved to a small house on Sleepy Creek. Rosa taught the farmers' wives needlework. The country women used coarse thread and made do with things they had because they were very poor but they did learn the stitches used in fine needlework. Rosa was very generous with her time and talent as well as money when she had it.

When Amma and her husband lived on North Washington Street, a black family lived three houses south and were referred to as "white folks" Johnson because they were clean, intelligent and had educated a daughter and two sons who became doctors. The Johnsons had come to Berkeley Springs as maid and coachman for Mrs. Suit. Mrs. Johnson told her that when they worked for Mrs. Suit, her husband slept in the little round tower below the road at all times. When there were no guests in the castle, Mrs. Johnson slept in the room with Rosa's children. With visitors, she slept on the flat roof or the tower room. Mrs. Johnson said she visited Rosa when she lived in the Rock Gap area in extreme poverty and asked if she had anything from her former life. Rosa went to a doorway under the stairs, dropped to her knees and brought out silver. She told Mrs. Johnson she never regretted her life, that she enjoyed it all rich or poor.

• In 2014, I had the good fortune to interview Mary Louise Miller Mayhew who was a child when she would go with her mother to visit Rosa regularly. "I can still see my mother and Rosa sitting there sipping tea," she recalled. It was about 1922 and the castle was long sold. Rosa was living in a boarding house on Fairfax Street. "She smoked," Mary Louise remembered. "And she crocheted clothes for my dolls."

Mary Louise's mother was devoted to Rosa. "We were the only ones of her friends who came to visit Rosa when she moved out to Sleepy Creek. Mother would bring her food."

She has recipes from Rosa. "She used Soult as the spelling of her name then," said Mary Louise.

The Miller family's connection with the castle did not end when Rosa moved away. Eugene Miller kept the keys to the castle to caretake for Mrs. Voorhorst during her tenure as a renter. "She was in Washington," said Mary Louise. "I would take the keys and June Heare and I would conduct tours for people."

When the Cunninghams owned the Castle during the 1920s and '30s, there were two kitchens. One was on the upper terrace and they made apple butter up there long before today's festival was even a glimmer of an idea.

There is no more fitting way to conclude this story of Berkeley Castle than to repeat a statement attributed to Rosa Suit. "There are so many stories about my castle and about my life there that you are at liberty to believe whatever pleases you most."

## ADDITIONAL INFORMATION

Published by High Street Press, Berkeley Springs, West Virginia

Distributed by the author.

Photo credits. Unless otherwise indicated, historic photos are from the collections of Betty Lou Harmison and the Museum of the Berkeley Springs. Contemporary photos are from Travel Berkeley Springs or the author.

Cover Photo: Berkeley Castle by Steve Shaluta, courtesy Travel Berkeley Springs.

Design & Production:

Ryan Harpster
ryan@silverbackdesigns.com

He and his wife Nici were the first couple to get married at the Berkeley Castle after Andrew Gosline opened his doors for public events.

# ABOUT THE AUTHOR

Jeanne Mozier lives in historic Berkeley Springs where she and her husband own and operate the Star Theatre, a unique vintage movie house. She is an award-winning writer of both fiction and nonfiction.

She has published six earlier books.

*Way Out in West Virginia, a must-have guide to the oddities and wonders of the Mountain State* was voted Best Book about West Virginia and Mozier was voted Best West Virginia Author by statewide readers. She wrote the text for two volumes of Steve Shaluta photographs: *West Virginia Beauty: Familiar and Rare* and *Wonders of West Virginia.*

Mozier co-authored the historical compendium *Images of Berkeley Springs* with Betty Lou Harmison.

She is also the author of *Panhandle Paradise*, the sole lifestyle guide to West Virginia's Eastern Panhandle.

Mozier published one novel *Senate Magic*, a political thriller that includes a magician who lives in Berkeley Castle.

Her short stories are included in three volumes of *Tales from the Springs*, and three of her plays have been staged. She was a contributor to the *West Virginia Encyclopedia*, and is a regular contributor of travel and lifestyle articles to a variety of regional and national publications.

A popular speaker, Mozier has received numerous awards for arts, tourism, business and volunteer activities including being named a West Virginia History Hero. She was one of five women in America honored by *Traditional Home* magazine as a Classic Woman. She chose to make West Virginia her home in 1977. Mozier is a graduate of Cornell and Columbia universities.

She can be contacted and this book
ordered by email at star@starwv.com
or by writing 3041 Pine Grove Rd.,
Berkeley Springs, WV 25411.

54380379R00034

Made in the USA
Charleston, SC
02 April 2016